Piano · Vocal · Guitar

ULTIMATE

Swing Standards

ISBN 0-7935-7705-5

HAL•LEONARD®
CORPORATION
7777 W. BLUEMOUND RD. P.O. BOX 13819 MILWAUKEE, WI 53213

Visit Hal Leonard Online at
www.halleonard.com

Contents

Ac-cent-tchu-ate the Positive

from the Motion Picture *HERE COME THE WAVES*

Lyric by JOHNNY MERCER
Music by HAROLD ARLEN

Moderately (with a steady rock)

Air Mail Special

By BENNY GOODMAN, JIMMY MUNDY
and CHARLIE CHRISTIAN

Across the Alley from the Alamo

Words and Music by
JOE GREENE

Bandstand Boogie

from the Television Series *AMERICAN BANDSTAND*

Words by BARRY MANILOW and BRUCE SUSSMAN
Music by CHARLES ALBERTINE

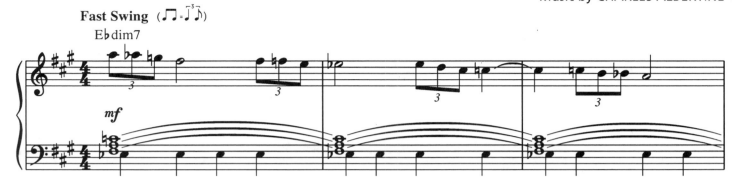

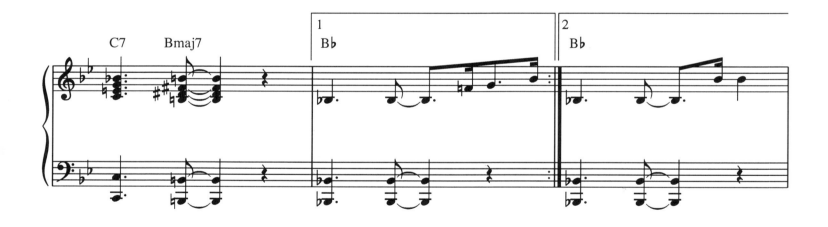

Beat Me Daddy, Eight to the Bar

Words and Music by DON RAYE,
HUGHIE PRINCE and ELEANOR SHEEHY

Medium Boogie Woogie

In a dink-y honk-y tonk-y vil-lage in Tex-as,

there's a guy who plays the best pi-an-o by far.

He can play pi-an-o an-y way that you like ___ it,

Between the Devil and the Deep Blue Sea

Lyric by TED KOEHLER
Music by HAROLD ARLEN

Blue Flame

Lyric by LEO CORDAY
Music by JAMES NOBLE and JOE BISHOP

Boogie Woogie Bugle Boy

from *BUCK PRIVATES*

Words and Music by DON RAYE
and HUGHIE PRINCE

MCA music publishing

Call Me

Words and Music by
TONY HATCH

MCA music publishing

Cherokee
(Indian Love Song)

Words and Music by
RAY NOBLE

Come Rain or Come Shine

from *ST. LOUIS WOMAN*

Words by JOHNNY MERCER
Music by HAROLD ARLEN

Christopher Columbus

Lyric by ANDY RAZAF
Music by LEON BERRY

Mis - ter Chris - to - pher Co - lum - bus, ___

Sailed the sea with - out a com -
He used rhy - thm as a com -

- pass; ___ When his
- pass; ___ Mu - sic

Ciribiribin

Based on the original melody
by A. PESTALOZZA
English Version by HARRY JAMES
and JACK LAWRENCE

The Continental

from *THE GAY DIVORCEE*

Words by CON CONRAD
Music by HERBERT MAGIDSON

Danke Schoen

Lyrics by KURT SCHWABACH and MILT GABLER
Music by BERT KAEMPFERT

A Cottage for Sale

Words by LARRY CONLEY
Music by WILLARD ROBISON

Cow-Cow Boogie

Words and Music by DON RAYE,
GENE De PAUL and BENNY CARTER

MCA music publishing

cow - boy __ song. __ It was a dit - ty he learned in the cit - y. __ "Cum - a - ti -

yi - yi ay, cum - a - ti - yip - it - tl - e - yi - ay," __ git a - long. _____ Git

hip, lit - tle dog-gies, git a - long. __ Bet - ter be on your way, __ git a - long. __

__ Git hip, lit - tle dog-gies, and he trucked __ 'em on down the

Daddy

Words and Music by
BOB TROUP

Medium bounce tempo

VOICE

Hey! lis - ten to my sto - ry 'bout_ a

gal named Dai - sy Mae_ La - zy Dai - sy Mae_

CHORUS

Do Nothin' Till You Hear from Me

Words and Music by BOB RUSSELL
and DUKE ELLINGTON

Moderately Slow

Drop Me Off in Harlem

Words by NICK KENNY
Music by DUKE ELLINGTON

Don't Get Around Much Anymore

Words and Music by BOB RUSSELL
and DUKE ELLINGTON

Everybody Loves My Baby
(But My Baby Don't Love Nobody But Me)

Words and Music by JACK PALMER
and SPENCER WILLIAMS

With a beat

VERSE

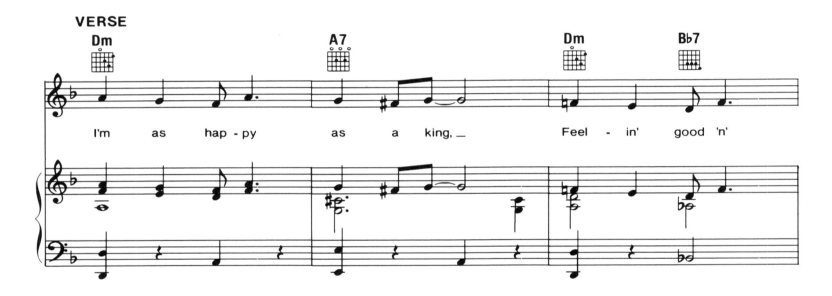

I'm as hap-py as a king, __ Feel-in' good 'n'

ev - 'ry-thing. __ I'm just like a bird in Spring, __

Flat Foot Floogie

Words and Music by SLIM GAILLARD,
SLAM STEWART and BUD GREEN

Moderato (*with swing*)

There's a new kill-er dil-ler There's a new har-lem thrill-er

A new way to ru-in the rugs A new dance for "Jit-ter Bugs."

Chorus

THE FLAT FOOT FLOOGEE with the Floy Floy THE FLAT FOOT FLOOGEE with the

* Pronounced so as to rhyme with "HOW"

Flying Home

Music by BENNY GOODMAN
and LIONEL HAMPTON
Lyric by SID ROBIN

Get Happy

from *SUMMER STOCK*

Lyric by TED KOEHLER
Music by HAROLD ARLEN

Hit the Road to Dreamland

from the Paramount Picture *STAR SPANGLED RHYTHM*

Words by JOHNNY MERCER
Music by HAROLD ARLEN

*Chord Names For Guitar

98

Heart and Soul

from the Paramount Short Subject *A SONG IS BORN*

Words by FRANK LOESSER
Music by HOAGY CARMICHAEL

Hey! Ba-Ba-Re-Bop

Words and Music by LIONEL HAMPTON
and CURLEY HAMMER

Honeysuckle Rose

from *AIN'T MISBEHAVIN'*

Words by ANDY RAZAF
Music by THOMAS "FATS" WALLER

Hooray for Love

from the Motion Picture *CASBAH*

Lyric by LEO ROBIN
Music by HAROLD ARLEN

How High the Moon

from *TWO FOR THE SHOW*

Words by NANCY HAMILTON
Music by MORGAN LEWIS

I Hear Music

from the Paramount Picture *DANCING ON A DIME*

Words by FRANK LOESSER
Music by BURTON LANE

I Thought About You

Words by JOHNNY MERCER
Music by JIMMY VAN HEUSEN

I'm Beginning to See the Light

Words and Music by DON GEORGE, JOHNNY HODGES,
DUKE ELLINGTON and HARRY JAMES

8vb

I've Got the World on a String

Lyric by TED KOEHLER
Music by HAROLD ARLEN

Mer - ry month of May, sun - ny

if I should ev - er let go, _____ I've got the

world on a string, _ sit - tin' on a rain - bow, Got the string a-round my fin -

- ger, what a world, what a _____ life, I'm in

love! _____ I've got the love! _____

Bell

I've Got You Under My Skin

from *BORN TO DANCE*

Words and Music by
COLE PORTER

If I Were a Bell
from *GUYS AND DOLLS*

Medium Bounce

By FRANK LOESSER

Ask me how do I feel__ Ask me now that we're co-sy and cling-ing__
how do I feel__ From this Chem-is-try les-son I'm learn-ing__

Well sir, all I can say__ is if I__ were a bell__ I'd be
Well sir, all I can say__ is if I__ were a bridge__ I'd be

ring-ing._____ From the mo-ment we kissed to-nite__
burn-ing._____ Yes, I knew my mor-ale would crack

I've Heard That Song Before

from the Motion Picture *YOUTH ON PARADE*

Lyric by SAMMY CAHN
Music by JULE STYNE

If You Can't Sing It
(You'll Have to Swing It)
from the Paramount Picture *RHYTHM ON THE RANGE*

Words and Music by
SAM COSLOW

In the Cool, Cool, Cool of the Evening

from the Paramount Picture *HERE COMES THE GROOM*

Words by JOHNNY MERCER
Music by HOAGY CARMICHAEL

Sue wants a bar - be - cue, Sam wants to boil a ham,
"Whee!" said the bum - ble-bee, "Let's have a ju - bi-lee!"

Grace votes for Bouil - la-baisse Stew.
"When?" said the prai - rie hen, "Soon?"

Jake wants a wee - ny bake,
"Shore!" said the di - no-saur.

steak and a lay - er cake, he'll get a tum - my-ache too.
"Where?" said the griz - zly bear, "Un - der the light of the moon?"

In the Mood

By JOE GARLAND

It All Depends on You

Words and Music by B.G. DeSYLVA, LEW BROWN
and RAY HENDERSON

I can be hap - py; I can be sad. I can be good or

I can be bad, it all de - pends on

you. _____ I can be lone - ly

Is You Is, or Is You Ain't

(Ma' Baby)

from *FOLLOW THE BOYS*

Words and Music by BILLY AUSTIN
and LOUIS JORDAN

MCA music publishing

It Could Happen to You

from the Paramount Picture *AND THE ANGELS SING*

Words by JOHNNY BURKE
Music by JAMES VAN HEUSEN

It Don't Mean a Thing
(If It Ain't Got That Swing)
from *SOPHISTICATED LADIES*

Words and Music by DUKE ELLINGTON
and IRVING MILLS

It's De-Lovely

from *RED, HOT AND BLUE!*

Words and Music by
COLE PORTER

*Pronounced "delukes"

It's Only a Paper Moon

Lyric by BILLY ROSE and E.Y. HARBURG
Music by HAROLD ARLEN

174

Jersey Bounce

Words by ROBERT WRIGHT
Music by BOBBY PLATTER, TINY BRADSHAW,
ED JOHNSON and ROBERT WRIGHT

They call it the Jer-sey Bounce, _____ A rhy-thm that real-ly counts _____ the tem-per-'ture al-ways mounts _____ where

No town _ makes it sound the same _ as where it came from! _ So if you don't feel so hot _____ Go out to some Jer - sey spot. _____ And wheth - er you're hep or not _ the Jer - sey Bounce - 'll make you swing. _ They _____

The Joint Is Jumpin'

from *AIN'T MISBEHAVIN'*

Words by ANDY RAZAF and J.C. JOHNSON
Music by THOMAS "FATS" WALLER

Tempo di-sturb de neighbors

They have a new ex-pres-sion a-long old Har-lem way____ that

tells you when a par-ty is ten times more____ than gay.____ To

say that things are jump-in' leaves not a sin-gle doubt ___ that

Juke Box Saturday Night

from *STARS ON ICE*

Words by AL STILLMAN
Music by PAUL McGRANE

The Lady is a Tramp

from *BABES IN ARMS*

Words by LORENZ HART
Music by RICHARD RODGERS

The Lady's in Love with You

from the Paramount Picture *SOME LIKE IT HOT*

Words by FRANK LOESSER
Music by BURTON LANE

Lean Baby

Lyric by ROY ALFRED
Music by BILLY MAY

Leap Frog

Music by JOE GARLAND

MCA music publishing

Let's Dance

Words by FANNY BALDRIDGE
Music by GREGORY STONE and JOSEPH BONINE

Let's Get Away from It All

Words and Music by TOM ADAIR
and MATT DENNIS

L-O-V-E

Words and Music by BERT KAEMPFERT
and MILT GABLER

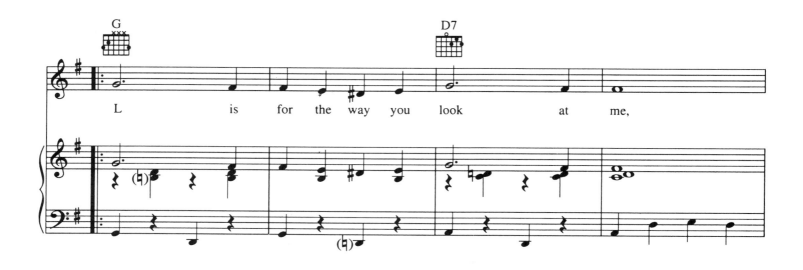

Love Is a Simple Thing

Words by JUNE CARROLL
Music by ARTHUR SIEGEL

Love Is Just Around the Corner

from the Paramount Picture *HERE IS MY HEART*

Words and Music by LEO ROBIN
and LEWIS E. GENSLER

Manhattan

from the Broadway Musical *THE GARRICK GAIETIES*

Words by LORENZ HART
Music by RICHARD RODGERS

We'll have Man-hat-tan   The Bronx and Stat-en   Is-land too;_____   It's love-ly
We'll go to Green-wich   Where mod-ern men itch   to   be   free;_____   And Bowl-ing
We'll go to Yonk-ers   Where true love con-quers   in the   wilds;_____   And starve to-
We'll have Man-hat-tan   The Bronx and Stat-en   Is-land too;_____   We'll try to

go - ing   through_____   the   Zoo;_____
Green you'll   see_____   with   me;_____
geth - er,   dear,_____   in   Childs'_____
cross Fifth Av -   en   ue;_____

Copyright © 1925 by Edward B. Marks Music Company
Copyright Renewed
International Copyright Secured   All Rights Reserved
Used by Permission

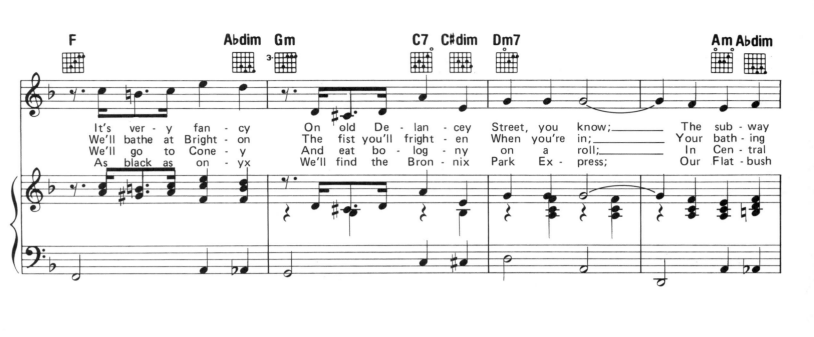

It's ver - y fan - cy On old De - lan - cey Street, you know;_____ The sub - way
We'll bathe at Bright - on The fist you'll fright - en When you're in;_____ Your bath - ing
We'll go to Cone - y And eat bo - log - ny on a roll;_____ In Cen - tral
As black as on - yx We'll find the Bron - ix Park Ex - press;_____ Our Flat - bush

charms us so,_____ When balm - y breez - es blow to and fro; And tell me what street
suit so thin_____ Will make the shell - fish grin Fin to fin; I'd like to take a
Park, we'll stroll_____ Where our first kiss we stole, Soul to soul; And for some high fare
flat, I guess_____ Will be a great suc - cess. More or less; A short va - ca - tion

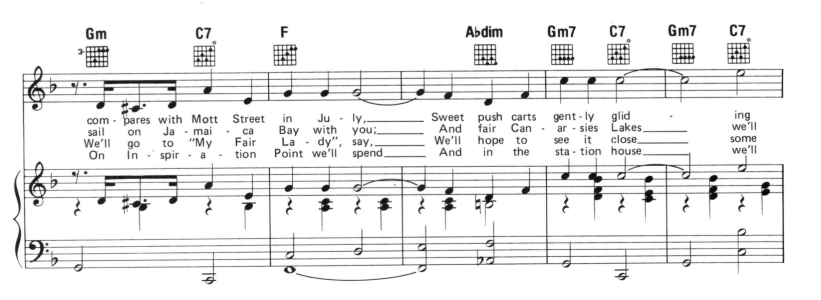

com - pares with Mott Street in Ju - ly,_____ Sweet push carts gent - ly glid - ing
sail on Ja - mai - ca Bay with you;_____ And fair Can - ar - sies Lakes_____ we'll
We'll go to "My Fair La - dy", say,_____ We'll hope to see it close_____ some
On In - spir - a - tion Point we'll spend_____ And in the sta - tion house_____ we'll

Mountain Greenery

from the Broadway Musical *THE GARRICK GAIETIES*

Words by LORENZ HART
Music by RICHARD RODGERS

On ___ the first ___ of May it ___ is mov - ing day.
Sim - ple cook - ing means more ___ than French ___ cui - sines.

Spring ___ is here, ___ so blow your job, throw your job a - way.
I've ___ a ban - quet planned which is sand - wich - es and beans.

Now's ___ the time ___ to trust to ___ your wan - der lust.
Cof - fee's just ___ as grand with ___ a lit - tle sand.

Moonglow

Words and Music by WILL HUDSON,
EDDIE DE LANGE and IRVING MILLS

Old Devil Moon

from *FINIAN'S RAINBOW*

Words by E.Y. HARBURG
Music by BURTON LANE

On the Sunny Side of the Street

Lyric by DOROTHY FIELDS
Music by JIMMY McHUGH

229

On a Slow Boat to China

By FRANK LOESSER

Satin Doll

from SOPHISTICATED LADIES

Words by JOHNNY MERCER and BILLY STRAYHORN
Music by DUKE ELLINGTON

Pick Yourself Up

from *SWING TIME*

Words by DOROTHY FIELDS
Music by JEROME KERN

But I'll be teach-er's pet yet, 'Cause I'm gon-na learn to dance or

burst.

She: Noth-ing's im-poss-i-ble I have found, for when my chin is

on the ground, I Pick my-self up, Dust my-self off,

Burthen
Polka-tempo

Rag Mop

Words and Music by JOHNNIE LEE WILLS
and DEACON ANDERSON

Chorus—*After 2nd and 5th Verses*

Saturday Night Is the
Loneliest Night of the Week

Words by SAMMY CAHN
Music by JULE STYNE

Scotch and Soda

Words and Music by
DAVE GUARD

Sentimental Journey

By BUD GREEN, LES BROWN
and BEN HOMER

Shoo Fly Pie and Apple Pan Dowdy

Lyric by SAMMY GALLOP
Music by GUY WOOD

Slow bounce

If you wan-na do right by your ap-pe-tite,__ If you're fus-sy a - bout your food,__ Take a

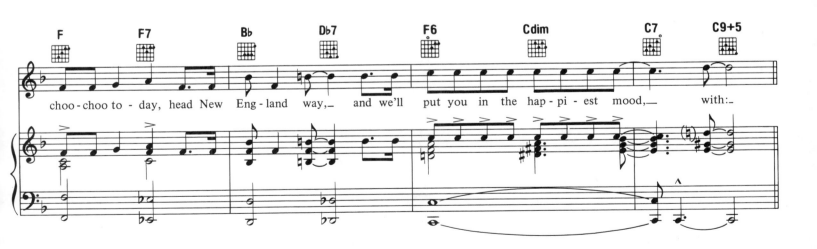

choo-choo to - day, head New Eng - land way,__ and we'll put you in the hap-pi - est mood,__ with:__

South of the Border
(Down Mexico Way)

Words and Music by JIMMY KENNEDY
and MICHAEL CARR

Sweet Sue-Just You

from *RHYTHM PARADE*

Words by WILL J. HARRIS
Music by VICTOR YOUNG

Stompin' at the Savoy

Words and Music by BENNY GOODMAN, EDGAR SAMPSON,
CHICK WEBB and ANDY RAZAF

Medium Swing Tempo

A String of Pearls

from *THE GLENN MILLER STORY*

Words by EDDIE DE LANGE
Music by JERRY GRAY

Swinging on a Star

from *GOING MY WAY*

Words by JOHNNY BURKE
Music by JIMMY VAN HEUSEN

T'ain't What You Do
(It's the Way That Cha Do It)

Words and Music by SY OLIVER
and JAMES YOUNG

Moderately

Tain't what you do, it's the way that cha do it. Tain't what you do, it's the
Tain't what you do, it's the way that cha do it. Tain't what you say, it's the

way that cha do it. Tain't what you do, it's the way that cha do it,
way that cha say it. Tain't what you say, it's the way that cha say it,

Take the "A" Train

Words and Music by
BILLY STRAYHORN

Tangerine

from the Paramount Picture *THE FLEET'S IN*

Words by JOHNNY MERCER
Music by VICTOR SCHERTZINGER

That Old Black Magic

from the Paramount Picture *STAR SPANGLED RHYTHM*

Words by JOHNNY MERCER
Music by HAROLD ARLEN

This Could Be the Start of Something

from *THE TONIGHT SHOW WITH STEVE ALLEN*

Words and Music by
STEVE ALLEN

Who knows what's writ-ten in the mag-ic book?
So keep your heart a-wake both night and day,

But when a
Be - cause the

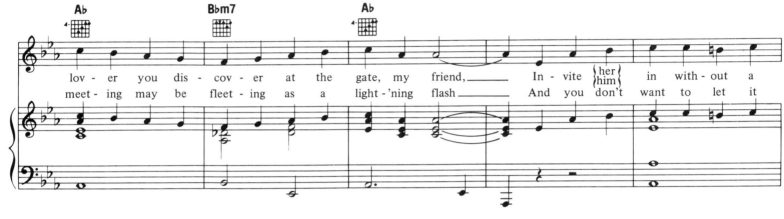

lov - er you dis - cov - er at the gate, my friend,_____ In - vite {her}{him} in with - out a
meet - ing may be fleet - ing as a light-'ning flash_____ And you don't want to let it

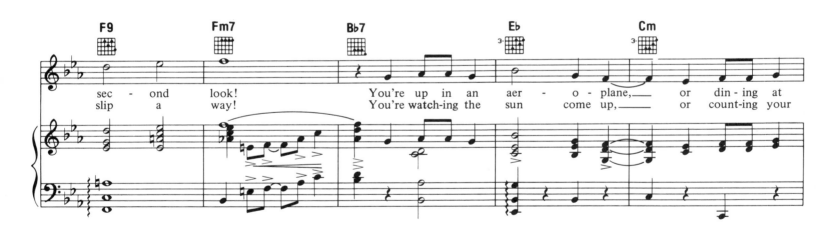

sec - ond look! You're up in an aer - o - plane,_____ or din - ing at
slip a way! You're watch-ing the sun come up,_____ or count-ing your

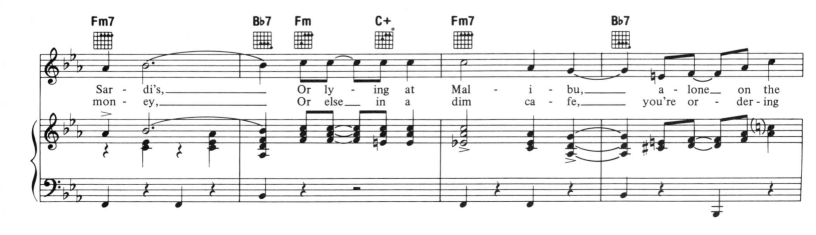

Sar - di's,_____ Or ly - ing at Mal - i - bu,_____ a - lone___ on the
mon - ey,_____ Or else in a dim ca - fe, you're or - der - ing

Thou Swell
from *A CONNECTICUT YANKEE*

Words by LORENZ HART
Music by RICHARD RODGERS

Tuxedo Junction

Words by BUDDY FEYNE
Music by ERSKINE HAWKINS, WILLIAM JOHNSON
and JULIAN DASH

Until the Real Thing Comes Along

Words and Music by MANN HOLINER, ALBERTA NICHOLS,
SAMMY CAHN, SAUL CHAPLIN and L.E. FREEMAN

Undecided

Words by SID ROBIN
Music by CHARLES SHAVERS

MCA music publishing

What a Diff'rence a Day Made

Lyric by STANLEY ADAMS
Music by MARIA GREVER

What a diff-'rence a day made, Twen-ty four lit-tle ho-urs,
Cuan-do vuel-va a tu la-do, No me nie-gues tus be-sos,

Brought the sun and the flow-ers, Where there used to be rain.
Que el a-mor que te he da-do, No po-drás ol-vi-dar.

My yes-ter-day was blue dear, To-day I'm part of
No me pre-gun-tes na-da, Que na-da he de ex-pli

Witchcraft

Lyric by CAROLYN LEIGH
Music by CY COLEMAN

Woodchopper's Ball

By JOE BISHOP
and WOODY HERMAN

Bright Boogie tempo

MCA music publishing

You Brought a New Kind of Love to Me

from the Paramount Picture *THE BIG POND*

Words and Music by SAMMY FAIN,
IRVING KAHAL and PIERRE NORMAN

Sweet one, _____ fair - er than the flow - ers, _____